HOW'S THE WEATHER?

It's Stormy!

Julie Richards

Smart Apple Media

This edition first published in 2005 in the United States of America by Smart Apple Media.

Smart Apple Media
1980 Lookout Drive
North Mankato
Minnesota 56003

Library of Congress Cataloging-in-Publication Data

Richards, Julie.
  It's stormy! / by Julie Richards.
  p. cm. — (How's the weather?)
  Includes bibliographical references and index.
  ISBN 1-58340-534-8 (alk. paper)
  1. Storms—Juvenile literature. [1. Storms. 2. Weather.] I. Title.
  QC941.3.R53 2004
  551.55—dc22   2003070414

First Edition
9 8 7 6 5 4 3 2 1

First published in 2004 by
MACMILLAN EDUCATION AUSTRALIA PTY LTD
627 Chapel Street, South Yarra 3141

Associated companies and representatives throughout the world.

Edited by Vanessa Lanaway
Page layout by Domenic Lauricella
Illustrations by Melissa Webb
Photo research by Legend Images

Printed in China

Acknowledgements
The author and the publisher are grateful to the following for permission to reproduce copyright material:

Front cover image: sheltering from a storm, courtesy of Reuters.

Reg Morrison/Auscape, p. 18; OSF/Auscape, p. 9; Digital Vision, pp. 7, 8, 21, 27; Getty Images/Image Bank, pp. 16; Photodisc, pp. 5, 10, 15, 23, 25, 26, 29; Photolibrary.com, pp. 11, 19, 28; Photolibrary.com/SPL, p. 6; Terry Oakley/The Picture Source, pp. 14, 22, 30; Reuters, pp. 1, 4, 17, 20.

While every care has been taken to trace and acknowledge copyright, the publisher tenders their apologies for any accidental infringement where copyright has proved untraceable. Where the attempt has been unsuccessful, the publisher welcomes information that would redress the situation.

Please note
At the time of printing, the Internet addresses appearing in this book were correct. Owing to the dynamic nature of the Internet, however, we cannot guarantee that all these addresses will remain correct.

Contents

How's the Weather?

Have you noticed how the weather always changes? You might feel warm sunshine or an icy wind, hear rain, or see lightning. Weather changes from day to day and **season** to season.

These people are sheltering from the storm.

A big lightning flash in a thunderstorm.

The weather varies from place to place, too. Some places have big storms nearly every day, while others have mostly clear weather. Most places have both storms and fine weather. How's the weather where you live?

5

Storms

Lightning is a giant electric spark that travels through the air. It can streak across the sky from cloud to cloud. Sometimes it leaps from the clouds down to the ground and back again.

Lightning streaking across the sky.

Lightning sometimes comes down to the ground.

Lightning is very hot. It heats the air as it travels through it. This makes the air **expand** with a flash and a loud noise. The noise that you hear is thunder.

7

A Stormy Day

On a stormy day, huge, black clouds block the sun. Thunder rumbles closer and closer. Your skin can feel tingly, and your hair might stand up. This is because of the electricity in the air around you.

A thunderstorm moves across the sky making everything dark.

Sometimes thunderstorms bring heavy rain and large **hailstones**. Most hailstones are quite small, but some can be huge.

Some hailstones are as big as baseballs.

Storm Safety

Always stay indoors during a storm, where you will be safe. Strong winds can blow trees over, and rain can make roads slippery.

Stay indoors during a thunderstorm.

Count slowly between lightning and thunder—
the higher you count, the farther away the
storm is.

Where Do Storms Come From?

Thunderstorms are made inside clouds called **cumulonimbus clouds**.

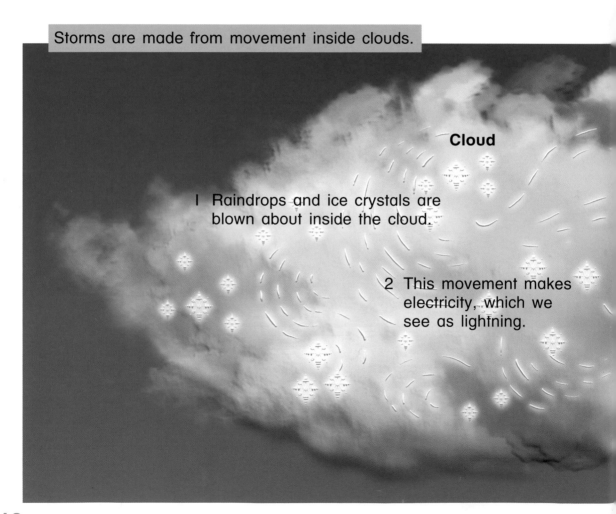

Storms are made from movement inside clouds.

Cloud

1 Raindrops and ice crystals are blown about inside the cloud.

2 This movement makes electricity, which we see as lightning.

Lightning and thunder actually happen at the same time. We see lightning before we hear thunder because light travels faster than sound.

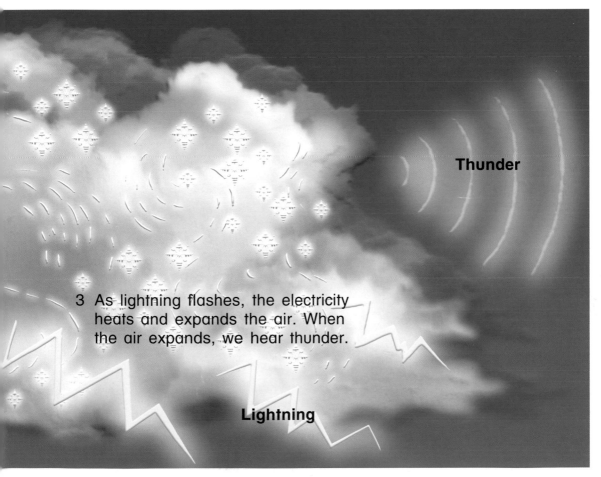

3 As lightning flashes, the electricity heats and expands the air. When the air expands, we hear thunder.

Thunder

Lightning

Stormy Seasons

Thunderstorms usually happen in late spring and summer. Rain from spring storms helps plants to grow into food for newly born animals. A summer thunderstorm can be refreshing at the end of a hot day.

Rain from this storm will help these plants grow.

Thunderstorms happen nearly every day in the wet season.

Places that have only a wet season and a dry season are hot all year. During the wet season, powerful winds called monsoons bring thunderstorms nearly every day.

15

Built for Storms

Tall buildings often have a pole called a lightning rod on their rooftops. Lightning is attracted to the lightning rod because it always follows the easiest path to the ground. This stops lightning from striking people in the streets below.

Lightning is attracted to the lightning rod on this building.

These workers are repairing powerlines after a big storm.

Powerlines and **substations** are built with special switches that turn off the power if lightning hits them. This is why your power sometimes goes off during a storm. The switches prevent fire or damage to the power equipment.

Useful Storms

Thunderstorms are useful because they make a gas called ozone. Ozone protects Earth from the sun's harmful rays. Lightning can start fires, which can be dangerous. However, fires can also keep forests healthy by clearing away dead trees.

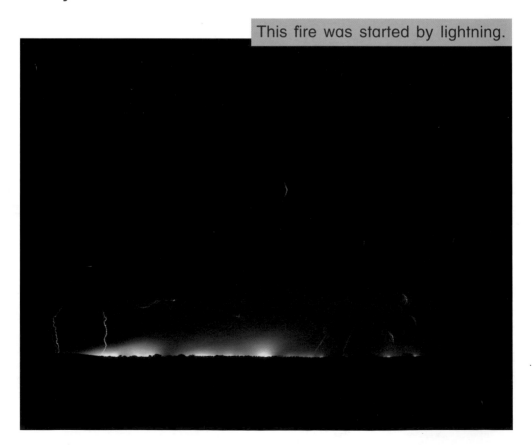

This fire was started by lightning.

This storm will help these crops grow.

Storms can help **crops** grow. Lightning heats up gases in the air and mixes them with rain. This mixture helps plants grow.

Dangerous Storms

Storms can be very dangerous. They bring fierce winds, heavy rain, and lightning. Strong winds can tear the roofs from buildings and pull trees from the ground.

A big storm caused this flood.

Storms can bring powerful winds.

Some big storms, such as hurricanes and tornadoes, bring very powerful winds that can damage cities. Some very dry places have dust storms. Strong winds whip dirt around, making it hard to see and covering everything with dust.

21

Cars, factories, and power stations send chemicals into the air, making it dirty. When the air is very dirty, heat gets trapped in Earth's **atmosphere**. This is called the greenhouse effect.

A blanket of dirty air stops some of the sun's heat from escaping Earth's atmosphere.

A very big storm has caused this damage.

Scientists believe that the greenhouse effect may cause bigger and more dangerous thunderstorms to happen. This means more floods and damage to buildings and crops.

Forecasting Storms

Scientists who **forecast** weather are called meteorologists. They use computers and look at **satellite** photos to see if storms are forming. This information is used to forecast weather.

Symbols on weather maps show us what kind of weather is coming.

Seattle
Great Falls
Boise
Minneapolis/St. Paul
Chicago
Boston
New York
San Francisco
Washington DC
Denver
Kansas City
Los Angeles
Phoenix
Atlanta
Dallas
New Orleans
Miami
Anchorage
Honolulu

Clouds	Rain	Snow	Storms	Sun	Wind

Satellites collect information about the weather.

Meteorologists use **radar** to look inside clouds and follow moving thunderstorms. If a big storm gets close to cities or towns, meteorologists can warn people about the danger.

Hurricanes and Supercells

Hurricanes and supercells are the most powerful storms on Earth. Hurricanes form over the ocean when smaller thunderstorms join together into one huge storm. They bring flooding rains and strong winds. Hurricanes can do terrible damage.

A hurricane is a huge swirling storm.

A tornado is the fastest spinning wind on Earth.

A supercell is a special kind of thunderstorm. The winds inside a supercell can spin so fiercely that they form a tube of air, called a tornado. Tornadoes can suck up objects as large as houses.

Stormy Sayings

People use weather sayings and words to describe everyday things.

It's a storm in a teacup.
This means that someone is making a big fuss over something very small.

Lightning never strikes twice in the same place.
People say this when they think something won't happen again.

The Empire State Building was once struck by lightning 12 times in one thunderstorm.

Weather Wonders

Did you know?

⭐ The stormiest place on Earth is Bogor, Indonesia. Out of 365 days, 322 are thunderstorm days.

⭐ About 2,000 thunderstorms are happening right now! Every day, there are about 40,000 thunderstorms across the world. Lightning strikes Earth one hundred times each second.

⭐ The least stormy place on Earth is the polar lands. Thunderstorms happen there only about once every ten years.

Try This!

Ask a parent or teacher for help.

Make lightning

⭐ Stand in a dark room with a partner.

⭐ Rub your feet back and forth on a piece of nylon carpet as fast as you can. Your partner must stand still.

⭐ Now touch your partner. What do you see? What do you feel?

Rubbing your feet very fast on the carpet has made a small amount of electricity. When you touch your partner, the electricity jumps from you to them just as lightning does.

Glossary

atmosphere	a blanket of gases surrounding Earth
crops	plants grown for food
cumulonimbus clouds	tall clouds that bring thunderstorms
expand	swell or get fatter
forecast	to know what kind of weather is coming
hailstones	frozen raindrops
radar	a way of looking at faraway objects
satellite	a small spacecraft that circles Earth
season	a part of the year that has its own kind of weather
substations	places that send electricity to homes

Index

Weather on the Web

Here are some Web sites that you might like to look at:
http://www.education.noaa.gov/sweather.html
http://www.fema.gov/kids/thunder.htm
http://www.kidslightning.info